.for.

Little Treasures

By Glenn Ridless

Illustrated by Jenny Faw

PETER PAUPER PRESS, INC.
WHITE PLAINS, NEW YORK

To my wife, Peggy

Copyright © 1990, 1991
Peter Pauper Press, Inc.
202 Mamaroneck Avenue
White Plains, New York 10601
ISBN 0-88088-733-8
Printed in China
14   13   12   11   10   9

LITTLE TREASURES

I had a chance to reach
the stars—
I touched the earth instead.

My body is a shell,
But my mind has no
boundaries.

I bought a motivational cassette
    tape on procrastination,
But I never got around to
    listening to it.

To look within,
One does not have to
    do without.

A label is easy to stick on,
But takes some effort
    to remove.

If you cry for what you
    don't have,
Then what do those who
    don't have cry for?

You can't judge a book by
  its cover,
But you can tell a lot
  by the first page.

A jigsaw puzzle is more
  challenging
When some of the pieces are
  missing.

Those who talk the loudest are
    invisible.
You can see right through them.

Once you stop acting like
    something
You become something.

It's easy to jump off the
    merry-go-round.
It's harder to stay on and
    not get dizzy.

If your heart can beat without
    thinking,
So can your mind.

First we want.
Then we get.
Then we wonder why we
    wanted it.
Then we get again.

Perfect balance is
Getting everything you want
    out of life
Without compromising any
    of your convictions.

Don't teach—don't preach—
don't try to reach.
Just seek and all will come
to you.

Acting does the opposite of
what you intend.
Instead of hiding, you become
transparent.

Did you ever notice that
sometimes a bad experience
Is funny when you look
back on it?

Put yourself on auto-pilot.

Drugs and alcohol make as
much sense as religion
and politics.

Fame does not make one an
authority.

We all lie.
The only difference is how we
   disguise it
To ourselves or to others.

If we were all brought up to
   think about the next
   generation,
This one would be just fine.

It used to be a compliment
to tell someone:
"You're a real human being."

Jealousy is by far the most
dangerous emotion.

We are all brothers and sisters
  in this world—
Unless we have to help
  one another.

Some people say I'm too
  negative.
I guess that makes them really
  positive.

Ever notice that people who say
"don't follow me"
Have thousands of people
following them?

If I could find just one square
inch on earth
Where I didn't have to answer
to anyone,
I would call that *Freedom*.

There are no new thoughts—
Just new ways to say them.

People will assume I had
    something to say
When really I had something
    to get rid of.

If I'm not responsible for the
   meaning of what I say
Then who is?

Without my sense of humor
I doubt I'd have much sense
   at all.

I've always tried to figure out
Why everyone tries to figure
each other out.

My speech is limited but my
thoughts are infinite.

Obsession is 99% of
accomplishing any goal.
1% is luck.

If we can imagine it, it can
come true.
So I suggest we be careful
about what we imagine.

We don't choose to be born.
We don't have the right to kill
  ourselves.
And yet I'm still searching for
  freedom.

Like money in the bank,
Patience breeds interest.

The most difficult action in the
    world
Is to listen.

The universe and the ego
    are very similar.
They never seem to end.

Do I really have something
   to offer,
Or do I really need something
   to give?

If I didn't care
I'd accomplish a lot more.

I'm not in harmony with
  myself
When what I feel on the
  inside does not show on
  the outside.

Unlike fine wine,
Bottled up emotions
Do not taste better with time.

Life is a struggle
For those who want more
than life itself.

There is quite a difference
between
Knowing and understanding.

If you spend your whole life
   searching for the truth,
You will either at one point
   become insane
Or end up becoming a liar
   yourself.

We are always acting even
   when we are alone.

I complain a lot and I have
    a lot of pain.
Yet if I took away the pain
I know that I would miss it.

All we are is all we think,
And we are limited by those
    who thought before us.

World peace is as silly as
    trying to land on the moon.
It's just a little farther away.

To really touch someone
    takes a lot more
Than just reaching out.

My mistakes have been my
   greatest heartache,
But I wouldn't be who I am
   without them.

It's impossible to judge
   someone
Without judging yourself.

I wanted to be a realist
Until I realized that was too
  idealistic.

If you like to poke fun at
  everyone,
Make sure you include
  yourself.

Perfection is the ugliest thing
in the world.

What is more challenging:
setting goals or reaching
them?

Every day is a chance to
    breathe.

All things do not need
    meanings.
Some things just are.

To find peace
One must go through a
   lot of noise.

An option is nothing
   more than
Two doors that are halfway
   open.

If I consider myself a magnet,
Then I am concerned with
   what I attract.

If we are all completely
   unique,
How can someone be better
   than another?

We are the parents of our
  parents
And the children of our
  children.

The best way to fight an evil
  man is to pay him no
  attention.

You might misplace your
   confidence,
But you can never lose it.

Those who claim to be my
   best friend
Are often my worst enemy.

Love at first sight
Does not last as long as
    developed love.

The heart is the only compass
    that can direct you
On the long journey to
    inner peace.

If I could think as slowly
as a tortoise walks,
I could move as fast as
a cheetah runs.

Most people think that all
they are is all they've been.

Those with something think
   I'm nothing
But even with nothing I'm
   still something.

Instead of building warships
We should build relationships.

The surest way to spread
   a message
Is to ask someone to keep
   it a secret.

I have no doubts that our
   world leaders
Are leading the world.
It's where they're leading
   it that I question.

I think at the end of time
God will have me fill out
  my own evaluation.

Children should look up to us
Only because they are shorter.

I cannot give you my love.
I can only share it.

The one with the most
    accusations
Is often the guilty party.

It is often what is not said
That causes an argument.

The concern we have for
   our environment
Should be proportional to
The concern we have for
   our children.

One man's hero
Might be another man's devil.

The color of my skin
Does not describe the me
   within.

A good marriage contains
Intimacy mixed with surprise
Bound together with loyalty.

There is not
Always tomorrow.

Why do we talk about
Our careers and possessions
More than our families?

I love all the people I meet.
It's liking them that I have
   trouble with.

There is no telling how far
One act of kindness will travel.

I strive to shut my eyes
And see and hear nothing:

Most of our plans in life
Are based on how much
attention we need.

My life will be over
When I run out of dreams.

The less I desire
The more freedom I have.

The more time I spend alone
The better I understand others.

My best friendships
Develop extremely slowly.

I pay my mortgage to God.
He is the owner of my house.

War makes no sense.
Winning does not outweigh
The incredible losses.

I finally turned around
    and realized
That you were behind me
    all the way.

Friends who argue
Sharpen each other's
Reasoning stones.

I never realized how addicted
    I was
Until I tried to stop.

Without a clock
Time becomes infinite.

The greatest leaders in the
    world
Have only led themselves.

Am I really here
Or am I in someone else's
    dream?

I do not feel alone in a crowd—
Only crowded.

If God does not exist,
It would not have harmed
   me one bit
To have believed in him.

I pity those who can see
And yet are still blind.

Honesty is not always
The most sensitive policy.

What I feed my body
Strengthens or weakens
my soul.

I married my wife for her
    qualities.
Her beauty was an extra bonus.

New technology takes us closer
    to the stars
And farther from ourselves.

I am amazed at how many
    experts on subjects
Are novices on life.

Accomplishing is easy.
It's figuring out what to do
That's the hard part.

It is better to lose a little face
Than to lose a lot of lives.

We are all terminally ill.

Not everything needs
an explanation.

It is sad when one's goals
Become something we must
    accomplish
Rather than something we'd
    like to accomplish.

An objective view
Can be a great communication
　　bridge.

There are many bodies,
But just a set amount of souls.

The more I learn,
The more I need to learn.

Each goal I reach
Allows me to set
A slightly higher one.

As a parent, I struggle with
My will to help my child vs.
Her need to be independent.

We expect more from others
Than we do from ourselves.

I can sleep easy
Near the sounds of the ocean.

I try to get an hour
Out of each minute of life.

Unfortunately, today people say
"I remember my first kiss,
    my first dance—
And my first marriage."

My warmest blanket
Is your daily love.

When I slow myself down
I speed up my awareness.

I have four basic needs:
Food, shelter, clothing,
    and you.

When I think of all the stars
  in the sky
And all the grains of sand
  on the earth,
My problems seem to fade
  away.

I am not God
So therefore I must accept
That I'll never be fully
  in control.

What I know now
Would in no way
Have helped me then.

Without my pen my thoughts
would remain just thoughts.